T0081175

GOOD

READER

Become a Good Reader!

Six Simple Steps

by Terri Heidger & Beth Stevens,
The Apron Ladies

Become a Good Reader! Six Simple Steps
By Terri Heidger and Beth Stevens

© Copyright 2016. Terri Heidger and Beth Stevens.
All rights reserved.

Cover and Interior Design: Charmaine Whitman
Design Elements: Shutterstock

Library of Congress Cataloging-in-Publication Data
Cataloging-in-Publication Data is on file with the Library of Congress.
978-1-4966-0530-6 (pbk.)
978-1-4966-0531-3 (ebook PDF)

Capstone Professional publishes professional resources for K–12 educators.
Contact us for tailored, in-school training or to schedule an author for a workshop or conference.
Visit www.capstonepd.com for free lesson plan downloads.

Maupin House Publishing, Inc. by Capstone Professional
1710 Roe Crest Drive
North Mankato, MN 56003
www.capstonepd.com
888-262-6135
proposals@capstonepd.com

Table of Contents

Introduction 4

1 Get Your Mouth Ready 8

2 Look at the Pictures 10

3 Chunk It by Looking for a Part You Know 12

4 Think about the Story 14

5 Read...Skip...Read...Skip...Then Go Back 16

6 Reread...Go Back and Read Again 18

Putting It All Together 20

Good Reader Strategy Class Profile 22

Good Reader Strategy Tiles 23

Introduction

We like to compare learning how to read to "doing a dance." And what a dance it is, as a child's eyes dart from page to strategy, cue, or clue and back again. The emerging and early reader is learning how to self-monitor word work by searching for, selecting, and applying structural or message strategies or sound or visual cues that will decipher meaning. Because you'll be repeatedly reinforcing these strategies, clues, and cues, you'll find that before long, it will take no more than a simple statement like "Get your mouth ready" for students to automatically know what to do.

This handbook puts the keys to "getting it" right at your fingertips. We teach and model these strategies every day. Modeling must take place during guided reading instruction, read alouds, whole group activities, and independent practice. It is very important to provide "visuals" for our students as we "think aloud" and continually model and practice as we teach. Of course, we must begin at a students' instructional level and continue to scaffold with more difficult text as our students' reading levels progress.

Using This Book

Students of all levels need to practice and apply these strategies while reading.

Once all the strategies have been introduced, we like to remind our students of the strategy (or strategies) that they are implementing during reading. Small strategy cards are useful to put in front of students as a visual reminder. Feel free to make a copy of the Good Reader Strategy Tiles at the end of the book. Cut out each strategy, and laminate it. Use these as visuals to remind students what strategy they are focusing on today in guided or independent reading.

The strategy tiles are also a great way to give the struggling reader the extra confidence they need to figure out the text. After a student has read the passage, place the strategy tiles that the student used in front of him or her. Watch as the student's face lights up when he or she knows exactly what strategies were used to figure out the text as he or she was reading. At the end of guided reading, give examples of a strategy used while reading. For example, "I saw several students today 'get their mouths ready' while 'looking at the pictures' to figure out tricky words."

Display the Good Reader Strategy Tiles in your classroom so students can reference them during independent reading, or make cards for their desks so they have easy access to them.

Questions and Activities

Throughout this book, the word **SAY** identifies those questions that model an appropriate strategy. These questions are related to deciphering the message of a text (meaning), recognizing familiar words and parts of words (visual), or making inferences (self-monitoring). You should ask your students these questions to help them hear their miscues and learn how to apply an appropriate Good Reader strategy.

The research-based strategies, clues, and cues in this book have been adapted from several respected sources, including Marie Clay, Tim Rasinski, Jean Feldman (Dr. Jean), and Debbie Miller. They were then refined and used by both of us in our classrooms. Each strategy is introduced and presented with a variety of enjoyable activities that reinforce it.

Monitoring Progress

Monitor student progress by using the Good Reader Strategy Class Profile on page 22. This tool will help you keep track of the strategies students are using. You will also find it useful for returning to a particular strategy a student may need to work on.

We know your students will be as pleased as ours are. Just as we do, you will find delight in hearing your students chant, "We get it!" or "We can read!"

Have fun as you adapt the activities to suit your own classroom. That's what good teachers do each and every day!

Good Reader Strategy Class Profile
22

Take the time to keep a class profile of the strategies that your students use during individual, partner, or guided-reading sessions. Put a check mark in the appropriate box when you note a student using the strategy. You can use this easy tool to diagnose student difficulties, assess progress, and guide your instruction. An objective tool like this is invaluable during parent conferences as well.

Student Name	1 Get Your Mouth Ready	2 Look at the Pictures	3 Chunk It by Looking for a Part You Know	4 Think about the Story	5 Read...Skip... Read...Skip... Then Go Back	6 Reread... Go Back and Read Again

① Get Your Mouth Ready

Students can eliminate wild guesses when they "get their mouth ready" by forming the initial or ending sound. Through the years, we have seen that this simple strategy allows the students to read the word instantly if they just "get their mouth ready" and say the sound.

Activities

CVC STRETCH

Before you begin this activity, select a CVC (consonant/vowel/consonant) word, such as *sat*. Model how to move a letter tile for each sound. Explain to students that the tiles are tools that allow us to stretch sounds into words. Place in front of the student the tiles for *sat* and demonstrate how to stretch the sounds into a word, using the tiles.

Visual Clue

SAY:

"Does that look right?"

"Get your mouth ready to say the first sound."

"Get your mouth ready to say the first sound and the last sound." (Don't worry: the middle sounds come later!)

"What would you expect to see if the word was _____?"

First sound out /s/, then /a/, and finally /t/. Who knew that tiles could have such powers!

Variation: Stretch out your arms from your body and create fists with both hands. Choose another CVC word, such as *toss*, and stretch out your arms with every letter.

HEADS OR TAILS?

On a medium-size rubber ball, use a permanent marker to draw the head of an animal on one side and the tail on the other. Call a student's name and say a CVC word, such as *cat*. Toss the ball to the student. The child gives the initial sound of the word if his or her thumb lands on the head and the ending sound if his or her thumb lands on the tail. Continue the game with other children as this reinforces beginning and ending sounds while eliminating the worry of having to know the middle sound.

MIRROR TALK

Divide the students into pairs, and give each pair a small, handheld mirror and a list of CVC words. Students will take turns giving each other words to pronounce as they look into the mirror. They can see exactly how to get their mouths ready and what their mouths should look like when they make that sound.

It is very important for a student to see how his or her mouth is formed while producing sounds at this stage of language development. Making that connection of the letter-sound relationship is key when you are teaching this strategy.

2 look at the Pictures

Looking at pictures gives students extra assurance before they guess at a word.

Visual Clue

SAY:

"What would you expect to see in a picture of _____?"

"Can you find the word that matches the picture?"

"Frame the word that matches the picture."

Meaning Clue

SAY:

"Look at the picture."

"What word would make sense here?"

"You said, '_____.' Does that word make sense here?"

"Skip it and go on…What word would make sense there?"

Activities

PICTURE-WORD SORT

Most teachers have an assortment of picture cards that accompany many of the reading programs. If you do not, you can use pictures from calendars. Be sure to ask your friends and family members to start collecting them for you. Each week, place at your centers at least five pictures and five vocabulary words used in the text you are reading. Have students match the pictures to the words. (Place colored dots on the backs of the pictures and the words so students can check that the colors match up. This way, it becomes a self-checking center.) Also provide blank index cards and crayons or colored pencils so that students can create their own illustrations and practice writing their favorite words.

VOCABULARY BOOKS

Give students a word that relates to a thematic unit. For example, if your topic is "Families," you might write words like "mother," "father," "sister," "grandmother," etc. In small groups or independently, have students select a word and illustrate it. You can create a class book or several small-group books of the illustrated words. Students can share books with the class and their families.

I'M AN AUTHOR NOW

Use wordless, take-home books that you have access to in your particular reading series. Ask students to write their own text for each page of the book. Have them match the illustrations and share their book for another reader to enjoy. This activity helps readers understand a story by using pictures in the book to make a movie in their minds.

3 Chunk It by Looking for a Part You Know

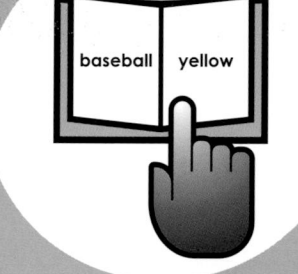

Students gain self-confidence to decode a word when they are able to identify a chunk within that word that they already know.

Activities

FRAME IT!

First, teach students how to frame chunks of a word by putting their two index fingers around the part within the word that they already know. Next, on the board or on sentence strips placed in a pocket chart, write out several big words that contain smaller, more familiar words. You can take words from books you are going to read to students.

Visual Clue

SAY:

"Do you see a part of the word that you know?"

"Can you chunk it?"

"Do you know a word that has the same chunk in it?"

"Can you find _____ inside that word?"

"Frame the part of that word that you already know."

For example, the word "hamburger" contains the words "am" and "ham."

If you are using sentence strips, you can also ask student volunteers to frame the smaller word chunk with finger puppets or "freaky fingers" (long plastic fingers available at party stores). Continue with volunteers until all words have been framed.

CAN YOU FIND IT?

Write several sentences on sentence strips placed in a pocket chart or taped to the floor. Make sure that each of the sentences includes at least one challenging word that contains a smaller, more familiar word. Note: You can take sentences from guided reading books or from science, social studies, or math texts.

Have all students read the sentences to themselves, and then ask for volunteers to read a sentence out loud to the class. Each reader should search for chunks within the larger words, framing his or her choices with pipe cleaners. Continue having volunteers search for chunks within larger words until all words have been framed.

SHOUT OUT!

This activity teaches students to automatically try to chunk a large and unfamiliar word using leveled readers and highlighting tape. As you read a book together as a class, find a larger word that can be chunked. Shout out, for example, "I see the word *in* on this page in a bigger word. Who can find it?" Students apply highlighting tape to the large word when they find it. Ask a volunteer to reread the sentence. Continue playing the game on each page of the leveled reading book to model and reinforce the chunking strategy.

4 Think about the Story

Context clues can help students figure out the meaning of a word they don't know in a story. This can help bring meaning to the entire passage and enable students to predict what might happen next. When we ask students to "think about the story," we are also asking them to predict what might happen before they read and as they read.

Activities

WHAT'S THE GIST?

Have your students orally read an unfamiliar text. If a student stumbles on a word, ask him or her to discuss the meaning. If unsure, he or she can use context clues and a prediction based on the text to determine meaning.

Meaning Clue

SAY:

"What can you try?"

"What are you checking to figure that out?"

"Try that again and think…"

"Does that look right?"

"Does that sound right?"

"Does that make sense in this story?"

"Look at the pictures. What do you think this might be about?"

"Make a prediction about what might happen."

LOOK, LISTEN, THINK

Make STOP signs with craft sticks and construction paper for each child. Explain that as you read a story out loud to them, you will be substituting a word that is nonsense or doesn't belong. Give students an example, such as "I saw a *migbus* at the beach." Ask them to hold up their signs when they hear the word that shouldn't be there.

Extend the activity by partnering students and having them read from their leveled readers. Partners read and try to stump each other by inserting words that don't make sense or are out of place in the story. This activity really encourages students to think about the story as they read and listen.

NEWSPAPER COVER-UP

Students can use book covers to help predict what might happen in a story. Using paper clips, cover the front of a Big Book with newspaper. Explain the importance of looking at a cover as a way to help predict what the story might be about. Tear off small pieces of the newspaper one at a time, pausing after each tear to invite students to predict what they think the story will be about. This activity helps students "put the pieces together" by making predictions based on each new tear as well as what previous tears revealed.

Continue reading the same Big Book. Stop at a word students may not know. Think aloud and model what you might do to gather meaning using picture cues, the text, and your background knowledge. Continue reading and ask students to "shout out" a word for which they do not know the meaning. Have them work together in pairs to figure out the meaning of the unknown word.

5 Read...Skip...Read... Skip...Then Go Back

Skipping an unknown word or words and then going back is a powerful strategy that helps a child use context clues to determine a word's meaning.

Activities

SKIP IT!

Before the lesson, cut out several construction-paper feet. Write one word of a phrase or sentence on each foot. Use at least one challenging word. Explain that as students read a sentence, they can skip a word they don't know and continue on. Tell them that sometimes when they do that, they can go back and figure out what the new word is.

Meaning Clue

SAY:

"Look at the picture."

"What would make sense?"

"You said, '_____.' Does that make sense?"

"Skip it and go on. What word would make sense there?"

Tape the feet to the floor to form a sentence or phrase, and invite a student to read it out loud as he walks on the words. Tell him or her to skip over an unknown word and continue to the end of the sentence. Encourage the student to make a guess about the unknown word after reading the whole sentence. Remind the student to use their other strategies to figure it out, too. Example: *The girl had a _____ in her sock, so you could see her toe.* (tear)

You also have the option of writing the sentences on a whiteboard. Your students can point and skip over the unknown word with a "magic wand."

LOOK, HOP, LEAP

Before the lesson, copy several different sentences from students' texts onto chart paper or sentence strips. Then have each student attach a frog sticker to a wooden craft stick. The students will use the frog to point to each word as they read. When they come to a word they do not know, they can use their frogs to "hop over" and skip the word and read on.

First, model this strategy using sentences with words students know. Then, model the activity with the whole class using sentences with challenging vocabulary. Encourage students to go back and read the sentence again using their context clues to attempt to read the unfamiliar word.

SING IT AGAIN!

Before the lesson, write your favorite poem or nursery rhyme on chart paper. It should be a rhyme that children are unlikely to know. Use sticky notes to cover key words in the poem or rhyme. For the lesson, enlist volunteers to read or sing the poem or rhyme, skipping over the words that are covered up with sticky notes. Then ask students to reread or re-sing the poem, this time with their guesses for what the covered words might be based on context clues. They then uncover the words to see if they have guessed correctly. Students absolutely love reading and rereading into a microphone! This activity also builds fluency, which is the bridge between decoding and comprehension.

6 Reread...Go Back and Read Again

Rereading a passage or page gives a curious reader another chance at figuring out new words. Rereading is also a valuable strategy for building fluency.

Activities

REREAD IT!

Review the Good Reader strategies. Use the tiles at the end of this book as reminders for students. Explain that good readers reread when they make a mistake in reading. Tell students that you are going to read a new book to them, but you will be making a mistake as you read. Ask them to listen for the mistake, cup their hands to their ears, and say

Clarifying/Monitoring

SAY:

"I like the way you tried to work that out. What did you do?"

"Were you right?" (Use this after both correct and incorrect responses.)

"Read it again to see if you were right."

"What did you notice? Why did you stop/hesitate?"

"Eh?" when they hear it. Then ask the whole class to say what the correct word should be. Model this a few times by hesitating, stumbling over a word, or substituting with a word that doesn't make sense.

PLAY IT AGAIN!

Children love to listen to themselves read. Ask each student to choose a favorite story to read into a tape recorder, using the same story each time they record. Try this activity at regular intervals during the year to give you a wonderful auditory portfolio. You'll be able to hear a child's progress! This is also a great way to share a child's progress with parents.

IT ONLY TAKES A MINUTE

Rereading…go back and read again is great for decoding words, but you can also use this strategy to improve fluency. After a student is familiar with a leveled-reader text, time him or her reading the text for one minute and chart the words correct per minute (WCPM). Chart each student's time,

recording his or her WCPMs in different colors each time to show individual progress. Repeat this exercise regularly. Students keep their charts in their own desks so that they can personally monitor their own progress and try to improve their WCPMs.

If you have tablets or other recording devices in your classrooms, your students might enjoy recording their reading into the device and listening to their fluency improve!

Putting It All Together

As our emergent readers develop into upper-emergent and early fluent readers, we need to constantly remind them to use their Good Reader strategies. They must consistently ask themselves these questions as they approach unfamiliar text: Does it look right? Does it sound right? Does it make sense?

As teachers, we can cue students as well as analyze their miscues. Are they using meaning or semantic cues? Are they using structure or syntactic cues? And are they using visual or graphophonic cues? Sometimes students only need to be reminded to "get their mouth ready" when they say *when* for *then* or *what* for *that*. This simple reminder helps our students to self-correct and rely upon the strategies taught to them.

Whether we model for our students Get your mouth ready; Look at the pictures; Chunk it by looking for a part you know; Think about the story; Read…skip…read…skip…then go back; or Reread…go back and read again, we are encouraging them to use all cues EQUALLY and not rely on the use of only one cue.

Be sure to ask yourself: *Do I model the strategies and behaviors that I want my students to acquire? Do I provide practice and reinforce my students' independent use of the strategies?* The Good Reader Strategy Class Profile on page 22 provides you with a useful tool to guide your teaching and assessment.

These Good Reader strategies work outside of language arts as well. Repeated reading *(Read…Skip…Read)* and rereading help students master the meaning of text and reinforce concepts in science, social studies, math, and other subjects.

Music is another technique that works for any subject area and, even more important, makes learning fun. Singing, chanting, and rhyming all improve fluency, phonemic awareness, oral language skills, and auditory memory.

We teach our students to "do the dance" by employing all the strategies and bringing meaning to the text—no matter the subject. That's what good readers do!

Good Reader Strategy Class Profile

Take the time to keep a class profile of the strategies that your students use during individual, partner, or guided-reading sessions. Put a check mark in the appropriate box when you note a student using the strategy. You can use this easy tool to diagnose student difficulties, assess progress, and guide your instruction. An objective tool like this is invaluable during parent conferences as well.

Student Name	① Get Your Mouth Ready	② Look at the Pictures	③ Chunk It by Looking for a Part You Know	④ Think about the Story	⑤ Read...Skip... Read...Skip... Then Go Back	⑥ Reread... Go Back and Read Again

Good Reader Strategy Tiles

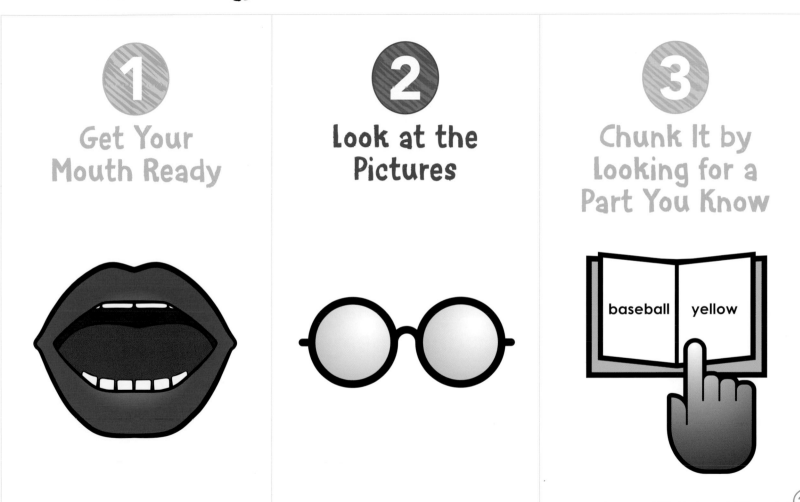

1 Get Your Mouth Ready

2 Look at the Pictures

3 Chunk It by Looking for a Part You Know

baseball yellow

Good Reader Strategy Tiles

4

Think about the Story

5

Read...Skip... Read...Skip... Then Go Back

6

Reread...Go Back and Read Again